My Sister Katie

My 6 Year Old's View
On Her Sister's Autism

By Mary Cassette
Illustrtations by Julie Robbins

AuthorHouse™
1663 Liberty Drive, Suite 200
Bloomington, IN 47403
www.authorhouse.com
Phone: 1-800-839-8640

AuthorHouse™ UK Ltd.
500 Avebury Boulevard
Central Milton Keynes, MK9 2BE
www.authorhouse.co.uk
Phone: 08001974150

First published by AuthorHouse 01/12/06

ISBN: 1-4259-0449-1 (sc)

Printed in the United States of America
Bloomington, Indiana

This book is printed on acid-free paper.

Bloomington, IN   Milton Keynes, UK

authorHOUSE

I would like to dedicate this book to my three beautiful daughters, Kacey, Katie and Kelly. You have made my life something magical, and I love you more than you will ever know. Also to my husband, Kevin. Without you I would never had made it this far, and you are my best friend. I would also like to thank my best girlfriend, Anne Marie, for being there for me through everything. Also to Carlie, for showing me there is always a way to accomplish your dreams. Julie, we always said we would publish a book, even if this isn't what we had in mind, here we are! And last but not least, thank you to the Cassette and Robbins family, for being the most supportive families any one could ask for. I love you all!

Hi. My name is Kacey. I like to cheerlead, tap dance, and play T-Ball. I have 2 sisters and I'm the oldest. My baby sister is Kelly. My other sister is Katie. She doesn't talk.

Katie and Kelly are a lot of fun to play with. Sometimes it's hard being the biggest sister. My mom asks for my help a lot. Sometimes I have to bring her a diaper for Kelly. Sometimes I have to buckel Katie in her car seat. Katie screams sometimes and tries to pinch me when she is mad. It hurts if she gets me.

My mom talked to me about Katie. She said Katie is autisitic. That is a hard word to say. Mom says that means Katie is different in some ways than me. She learns differently and thinks differently. There is a lot that she doesn't understand yet. That is why she doesn't talk, but she is trying.

Katie goes to a special school and has her own teacher. I asked mom if Katie will go to my school when she gets big. She said she doesn't know. She said kids who are autistic are not all the same as other autistic kids. Some can talk and go to my school but need a special helper.

Sometimes they play differently and sometimes they want to play all by themselves. When Katie was little she would not stack blocks up high, she would only line them up straight. Mom says most autistic kids like to do things the same way all the time. They don't like changes in their routine. Katie got mad on the bus when they took her home a different way.

Others might talk just a little so they go to a special school like Katie. Some wave their hands around or rock in their chair. Some are very loud and some are very quiet. Some don't like kisses or hugs or friends. Katie likes kisses and hugs.

I don't like it when Katie screams or tries to pull my hair. Daddy told me she does that because she is frustrated. She doesn't know how to talk and when she gets mad she doesn't know what else to do. She does not understand some things so we have to be patient with her.

Daddy says I can help everyone by looking out for my sisters and making sure they are safe. He said I shouldn't force Katie to do things she doesn't want to because some autistic kids don't like to be held too tight or looked at too long. Sometimes they don't like the fell of things or to touch things. That means I have to see how Katie reacts and help her to be happy.

Mom says that everyone is different in their own way. She says we need to be nice to everyone and not stare or make them feel bad if they walk funny or talk funny. Or if they don't talk at all like Katie. Mom says it's not nice to point at people, but it's nice to wave and say "Hi!"

I wonder what Katie will do when she grows up. Mom says she gets scared when she thinks about it. She says when autistic kids grow up some get jobs and some live at home with their moms and dads. She says we will just have to wait and see what Katie will do.

I saw my mom cry yesterday. I asked her what was wrong and she said she was sad about Katie. Most of the time my mom is very happy and proud of me and Katie and Kelly. But yesterday I gave her a hug and told her not to be sad.

Katie is a lot of fun. She is very pretty and likes to laugh. I am glad she is my sister, even if I get mad at her sometimes. Mom says she is proud of me for being such a good sister to Katie. I love Katie very much.